9/11: America's Day of Terror and Resilience

American history, Volume 15

Michael Johnson

Published by Harmony House Publishing, 2024.

While every precaution has been taken in the preparation of this book, the publisher assumes no responsibility for errors or omissions, or for damages resulting from the use of the information contained herein.

9/11: AMERICA'S DAY OF TERROR AND RESILIENCE

First edition. April 5, 2024.

Copyright © 2024 Michael Johnson.

ISBN: 979-8224975877

Written by Michael Johnson.

Table of Contents

"To the memory of the lives lost on that fateful day, and to the resilience of the survivors and their families,

This book is dedicated to all those who were forever changed by the events of September 11, 2001. To the brave first responders who risked their lives to save others, to the ordinary citizens who showed extraordinary courage in the face of unimaginable tragedy, and to the families who continue to carry the weight of loss and grief.

May their stories of resilience and unity serve as a beacon of hope and inspiration in our collective journey toward healing and peace.

With deepest respect and remembrance,

Michael Johnson"

Chapter 1: Prelude to Tragedy

In the bright, optimistic years leading up to September 11, 2001, the world seemed poised on the brink of a new era. However, beneath the surface of global prosperity and technological advancement, tensions simmered, particularly in the volatile regions of the Middle East. This chapter delves into the complex web of events, ideologies, and geopolitical maneuvering that set the stage for the most devastating terrorist attack in history.

The Political Climate:

The political landscape of the late 20th century was marked by the end of the Cold War and the emergence of the United States as the world's sole superpower. However, the dissolution of the Soviet Union did not bring about a new era of peace and stability. Instead, it ushered in a period of uncertainty and realignment as nations jostled for power and influence on the world stage.

In the Middle East, decades of conflict and instability had left deep scars on the region. The Israeli-Palestinian conflict remained unresolved, fueling resentment and violence on both sides. Meanwhile, authoritarian regimes ruled over much of the Arab world, suppressing dissent and breeding radicalism. One such regime was that of Saddam Hussein in Iraq, whose aggressive actions and pursuit of weapons of mass destruction put him on a collision course with the West.

At the same time, a new form of extremism was taking root in the Islamic world. Inspired by a radical interpretation of Islam, groups like al-Qaeda sought to challenge what they saw as the corrupt and oppressive influence of Western powers. Led by Osama bin Laden, al-Qaeda attracted followers from across the Muslim world and beyond, preaching a message of jihad against America and its allies.

Key Figures and Organizations:

1. Osama bin Laden: Born into a wealthy Saudi family, Osama bin Laden was radicalized by the Soviet invasion of Afghanistan in the 1980s. He went on to found al-Qaeda, the terrorist organization responsible for the September 11

attacks. Bin Laden's charisma and wealth made him a powerful figure in the jihadist movement, and his calls for holy war resonated with disaffected Muslims around the world.

2. Ayman al-Zawahiri: A longtime associate of bin Laden, Ayman al-Zawahiri played a key role in shaping al-Qaeda's ideology and strategy. As the group's chief ideologue and strategist, al-Zawahiri was instrumental in planning the September 11 attacks. His background as a physician and his intellectual prowess made him a respected figure within jihadist circles.

3. The Taliban: Originally formed as a movement to restore order to war-torn Afghanistan, the Taliban emerged as a powerful force in the country in the 1990s. With their strict interpretation of Islamic law and support for al-Qaeda, the Taliban provided a safe haven for bin Laden and his followers. Their refusal to hand over bin Laden to the United States would ultimately lead to war.

4. The CIA and Intelligence Community: On the other side of the conflict, the Central Intelligence Agency and other intelligence agencies played a crucial role in tracking and disrupting terrorist networks. However, bureaucratic infighting and a lack of coordination hampered their efforts, allowing groups like al-Qaeda to operate with relative impunity.

Events Leading Up to September 11, 2001:

As tensions simmered in the Middle East, the stage was set for a catastrophic confrontation between radical Islamists and the West. In February 1993, a group of terrorists linked to al-Qaeda detonated a truck bomb in the parking garage of the World Trade Center in New York City, killing six people and injuring over a thousand. While the attack failed to bring down the towers, it served as a chilling warning of the threat posed by Islamist extremists.

Throughout the 1990s, al-Qaeda continued to carry out attacks against American interests around the world, including the bombings of U.S. embassies in Kenya and Tanzania in 1998, which killed over 200 people. Meanwhile, tensions between the United States and Iraq escalated following the Gulf War, as Saddam Hussein's regime defied international sanctions and obstructed weapons inspections.

In the summer of 2001, intelligence agencies began to pick up ominous signs of an impending attack. Reports of increased chatter among al-Qaeda operatives raised concerns of a major strike against American targets. However, a series of intelligence failures and miscommunications prevented the dots from being connected in time to prevent the tragedy that would unfold on the morning of September 11th.

Conclusion:

As the world watched in horror on that fateful day, it became clear that the events of September 11, 2001, were not merely a random act of violence, but the culmination of years of simmering tensions and ideological conflict. In the chapters that follow, we will delve deeper into the events of that day and their far-reaching consequences, exploring the heroism, tragedy, and resilience that defined America's response to the deadliest terrorist attack in history.

Chapter 2: The Morning of September 11

The morning of September 11, 2001, began like any other day for millions of people across the United States. However, within a matter of hours, the world would be forever changed by a series of coordinated terrorist attacks that would claim thousands of lives and alter the course of history.

Timeline of Events Leading Up to the Attacks:

5:45 AM - Hijackers Mohamed Atta and Abdulaziz al-Omari board American Airlines Flight 11 at Boston's Logan International Airport. Atta is seated in 8D, while al-Omari is in 8G.

7:59 AM - American Airlines Flight 11, a Boeing 767 bound for Los Angeles with 92 people on board, takes off from Logan International Airport. Among the passengers are five hijackers, led by Mohamed Atta.

8:14 AM - United Airlines Flight 175, also bound for Los Angeles, takes off from Boston's Logan International Airport with 65 passengers on board. Five hijackers, including Marwan al-Shehhi, are on board.

8:19 AM - Flight attendants on American Airlines Flight 11 begin making routine announcements to passengers. Meanwhile, the hijackers storm the cockpit and take control of the aircraft.

8:20 AM - American Airlines Flight 77, a Boeing 757 en route from Washington Dulles International Airport to Los Angeles, takes off with 64 passengers on board. Five hijackers, including Hani Hanjour, are on board.

8:42 AM - United Airlines Flight 93, a Boeing 757 en route from Newark International Airport to San Francisco, takes off with 44 passengers on board. Four hijackers, led by Ziad Jarrah, are on board.

8:46 AM - American Airlines Flight 11 crashes into the North Tower of the World Trade Center in New York City, traveling at approximately 470 miles per hour. The impact creates a gaping hole between the 93rd and 99th floors.

8:47 AM - News networks begin reporting on the crash at the World Trade Center, initially believing it to be a tragic accident.

9:03 AM - United Airlines Flight 175 crashes into the South Tower of the World Trade Center, striking between the 77th and 85th floors at approximately

590 miles per hour. The impact is captured live on television, shocking viewers around the world.

9:08 AM - The Federal Aviation Administration (FAA) bans all takeoffs of flights going to or through New York City airspace.

9:21 AM - The Port Authority of New York and New Jersey orders the evacuation of all bridges and tunnels in the New York City area.

9:28 AM - The FAA bans all takeoffs nationwide, effectively shutting down the airspace over the United States.

9:37 AM - American Airlines Flight 77 crashes into the Pentagon, causing extensive damage and loss of life.

9:42 AM - The United States Capitol and the White House are evacuated as a precautionary measure.

9:59 AM - The South Tower of the World Trade Center collapses, sending a plume of smoke and debris cascading through the streets of Lower Manhattan.

10:03 AM - United Airlines Flight 93 crashes into a field near Shanksville, Pennsylvania, after passengers attempt to regain control of the aircraft from the hijackers.

10:28 AM - The North Tower of the World Trade Center collapses, marking the end of the deadliest terrorist attack in history.

Initial Reactions and Confusion as the Situation Unfolds:

As news of the attacks spread, confusion and disbelief gripped the nation. In New York City, eyewitnesses described scenes of chaos and panic as people fled the burning towers and emergency responders rushed to the scene. In Washington, D.C., government officials grappled with the unfolding crisis, scrambling to assess the extent of the damage and coordinate a response.

For many Americans, the attacks on September 11th were a surreal and incomprehensible tragedy. As images of the burning towers and collapsing buildings flashed across television screens, millions of people struggled to make sense of what was happening. In the absence of concrete information, rumors and speculation ran rampant, fueling fear and uncertainty.

In the days and weeks that followed, the full scale of the devastation became clear. Nearly 3,000 people had lost their lives in the attacks, including office workers, first responders, and passengers aboard the hijacked planes. The attacks had also dealt a crippling blow to the nation's sense of security, prompting a massive overhaul of the country's counterterrorism efforts and reshaping the geopolitical landscape for years to come.

Conclusion:

The morning of September 11, 2001, was a day that would be etched into the collective memory of a generation. From the initial shock of the hijackings to the horror of the attacks themselves, the events of that fateful morning would leave an indelible mark on the world. In the chapters that follow, we will explore the human stories behind the headlines, from the heroism of the first responders to the resilience of the survivors, as we seek to understand the true impact of 9/11 on America and the world.

Chapter 3: The World Trade Center

Background on the World Trade Center Complex:

The World Trade Center (WTC) complex, located in Lower Manhattan, New York City, was a symbol of economic power and modernity. Designed by architect Minoru Yamasaki and completed in 1973, the Twin Towers—known as the North Tower (1 WTC) and the South Tower (2 WTC)—stood as the tallest buildings in the world at the time of their completion. Rising to a height of 1,368 and 1,362 feet respectively, the towers were comprised of steel frames and covered in aluminum alloy skin, featuring a unique design of narrow windows and distinctive facades.

The complex encompassed seven buildings, including the iconic Twin Towers, as well as the Marriott World Trade Center hotel (3 WTC), the Vista Hotel (5 WTC), and the World Trade Center Plaza. The Towers were not only office spaces but also a bustling hub of activity, hosting businesses, government offices, restaurants, and observation decks that offered panoramic views of the city.

The World Trade Center quickly became an integral part of the New York City skyline, a symbol of economic prowess and urban modernity. It served as a global financial center, attracting businesses and workers from around the world. However, this iconic symbol of American prosperity would soon become the target of one of the deadliest terrorist attacks in history.

Detailed Description of the Attacks on the Twin Towers:

On the morning of September 11, 2001, American Airlines Flight 11, hijacked by terrorists, crashed into the North Tower of the World Trade Center at 8:46 AM EDT. The impact of the Boeing 767, traveling at approximately 470 miles per hour, created a massive fireball and a gaping hole between the 93rd and 99th floors of the tower. The force of the impact instantly killed all 92 people on board the plane and ignited a raging inferno within the building.

As the world watched in horror, news cameras captured the smoke billowing from the North Tower and the frantic efforts of first responders to evacuate those trapped inside. Office workers above the impact zone faced a harrowing choice—stay put and await rescue, or attempt to navigate the treacherous stairwells to safety. Many chose the latter, descending hundreds of floors amidst choking smoke and debris.

Meanwhile, just 17 minutes after the first impact, United Airlines Flight 175, also hijacked by terrorists, crashed into the South Tower of the World Trade Center at 9:03 AM EDT. The Boeing 767 struck the tower between the 77th and 85th floors, traveling at approximately 590 miles per hour. The impact was captured live on television, shocking viewers around the world and deepening the sense of disbelief and horror.

The South Tower's structural integrity was severely compromised by the impact, and fires raged out of control on multiple floors. Despite the heroic efforts of first responders and building personnel, the situation quickly deteriorated as the fire spread and the building began to sway. At 9:59 AM EDT, just 56 minutes after being struck, the South Tower collapsed in a cascade of twisted steel and concrete, sending a plume of smoke and debris cascading through the streets of Lower Manhattan.

Stories of Survival and Heroism Amidst the Chaos:

Amidst the chaos and destruction of September 11th, stories of survival and heroism emerged from the rubble of the World Trade Center. From the bravery of first responders to the selflessness of ordinary citizens, these tales of courage and resilience served as beacons of hope in the darkest of times.

One such story is that of Rick Rescorla, the head of security for Morgan Stanley, whose quick thinking and leadership saved the lives of over 2,700 employees in the South Tower. Despite being ordered to stay put after the first plane struck the North Tower, Rescorla ignored the directive and began evacuating his colleagues from their offices on the 44th floor. With his calm demeanor and authoritative presence, Rescorla guided his team to safety, singing songs and cracking jokes to keep spirits high amidst the chaos. Tragically, Rescorla himself perished in the collapse of the South Tower, but his bravery and sacrifice saved countless lives that day.

Another tale of heroism comes from the passengers aboard United Airlines Flight 93, which was hijacked by terrorists en route from Newark to San Francisco. Through a combination of quick thinking and sheer determination, the passengers and crew of Flight 93 managed to overpower the hijackers and prevent the plane from reaching its intended target—likely the White House or the U.S. Capitol. In a final act of defiance, the passengers stormed the cockpit and engaged in a desperate struggle for control of the aircraft. At 10:03 AM EDT, Flight 93 crashed into a field near Shanksville, Pennsylvania, killing all 44 people on board but sparing countless others from a similar fate.

As the dust settled and the enormity of the tragedy became clear, the stories of survival and heroism that emerged from the World Trade Center served as a reminder of the resilience of the human spirit in the face of unimaginable adversity. In the chapters that follow, we will continue to explore the impact of 9/11 on America and the world, and the enduring legacy of those who lost their lives on that fateful day.

Chapter 4: The Pentagon

Overview of the Attack on the Pentagon:

While the attacks on the World Trade Center towers in New York City dominated the headlines on September 11, 2001, another target of the terrorist hijackers was the Pentagon, the headquarters of the United States Department of Defense. At 9:37 AM EDT, American Airlines Flight 77, a Boeing 757 en route from Washington Dulles International Airport to Los Angeles, crashed into the western side of the Pentagon, the symbol of American military power.

The impact of Flight 77 caused a catastrophic explosion, tearing through three of the Pentagon's five concentric rings and igniting a massive fire that raged for hours. The force of the impact and subsequent fireball killed all 64 passengers on board the plane, as well as 125 military and civilian personnel inside the Pentagon, making it the deadliest event of the day outside of New York City.

The attack on the Pentagon sent shockwaves through the nation's capital and raised fears of further coordinated strikes against other key government buildings. It also underscored the vulnerability of even the most heavily fortified military installations to terrorist attacks, prompting a reevaluation of security protocols and emergency response procedures.

Profiles of Individuals Impacted by the Attack:

The attack on the Pentagon claimed the lives of individuals from diverse backgrounds and walks of life, each with their own stories of service, sacrifice, and heroism.

- Barbara Olson: A prominent conservative commentator and attorney, Barbara Olson was a passenger aboard American Airlines Flight 77. Using an airphone, Olson called her husband, Solicitor General Theodore Olson, and informed him of the hijacking. Despite the chaos and confusion, Olson remained calm and composed, providing crucial information to authorities about the unfolding situation. Her courage and determination in the face of danger serve as a testament to the resilience of the human spirit.

- Charles Burlingame: A retired Navy pilot and captain of American Airlines Flight 77, Charles Burlingame was one of the 64 people killed in the attack on the Pentagon. Burlingame had served as a fighter pilot in the Vietnam War before joining American Airlines as a commercial pilot. His tragic death underscored the indiscriminate nature of terrorism and the profound impact it can have on individuals and their families.

- Cheryl McNair: A civilian employee of the Department of the Army, Cheryl McNair was working at her desk in the Pentagon when Flight 77 struck the building. McNair, an accomplished pianist and music teacher, was known for her warm personality and dedication to her work. Her loss was deeply felt by her colleagues and loved ones, who remembered her as a compassionate and talented individual.

These are just a few of the many individuals who lost their lives in the attack on the Pentagon. Their stories serve as a poignant reminder of the human toll of terrorism and the sacrifices made by those who serve their country.

Response Efforts and Rescue Operations at the Pentagon:

In the immediate aftermath of the attack, first responders and emergency personnel sprang into action, rushing to the scene to extinguish fires, treat the injured, and search for survivors. Despite the chaos and destruction, their swift and coordinated response saved numerous lives and prevented further loss of life.

Firefighters from Arlington County and surrounding jurisdictions battled intense flames and thick smoke as they worked to contain the blaze and prevent it from spreading to other parts of the Pentagon. Using specialized equipment and techniques, they conducted search and rescue operations in the unstable and hazardous environment, risking their own safety to save others.

Meanwhile, military personnel and civilian volunteers formed ad hoc triage centers to treat the injured and provide medical assistance to those in need. Improvised stretcher teams carried wounded survivors from the burning building to waiting ambulances, where they were transported to nearby hospitals for further treatment.

As the day wore on, additional resources and personnel were mobilized to support the ongoing rescue and recovery efforts at the Pentagon. The Federal

Emergency Management Agency (FEMA), the American Red Cross, and other federal agencies provided logistical support, medical supplies, and counseling services to survivors and their families.

Despite the challenges posed by the extensive damage and hazardous conditions, the response efforts at the Pentagon were marked by courage, professionalism, and teamwork. The selfless actions of first responders and volunteers in the aftermath of the attack exemplified the spirit of resilience and solidarity that would come to define America's response to the events of September 11th.

Conclusion:

The attack on the Pentagon on September 11, 2001, was a tragic and sobering reminder of the vulnerability of even the most fortified military installations to acts of terrorism. The loss of life and destruction caused by the attack underscored the profound impact of terrorism on individuals, families, and communities.

In the chapters that follow, we will continue to explore the aftermath of 9/11, including the long-term effects on national security, the ongoing efforts to prevent future attacks, and the enduring legacy of those who lost their lives on that fateful day.

Chapter 5: Flight 93: The Heroes of Shanksville

Narrative of the Hijacking and Crash of Flight 93:

On the morning of September 11, 2001, United Airlines Flight 93, a Boeing 757 en route from Newark International Airport to San Francisco, was hijacked by four terrorists. The hijackers were affiliated with the al-Qaeda terrorist network, and their plan was to use Flight 93 as a weapon to target a prominent landmark in Washington, D.C., likely either the White House or the U.S. Capitol.

The flight took off from Newark at 8:42 AM EDT, with 44 passengers and crew on board. Among the passengers were businessmen, vacationers, and families traveling for various reasons. Little did they know that their flight would soon become a battleground between the hijackers and a group of courageous passengers who would ultimately thwart the terrorists' plans.

Approximately 46 minutes into the flight, the hijackers stormed the cockpit and seized control of the aircraft, using makeshift weapons to subdue the crew and passengers. They announced their intentions to the passengers over the intercom, threatening to crash the plane unless their demands were met.

In the chaos and confusion that followed, a group of passengers, led by individuals like Todd Beamer, Jeremy Glick, Mark Bingham, and Tom Burnett, realized the gravity of the situation and began to formulate a plan to confront the hijackers and regain control of the aircraft. Armed with nothing but their courage and determination, these ordinary individuals rose to the occasion and prepared to make the ultimate sacrifice to save others.

As the hijackers piloted the plane towards its intended target in Washington, D.C., the passengers and crew of Flight 93 launched a daring counterattack. They rushed the cockpit, engaging in a fierce struggle with the hijackers for control of the aircraft. Despite the odds stacked against them, they fought bravely, knowing that their actions could mean the difference between life and death for countless others on the ground.

In the final moments of the flight, the hijackers, realizing that they were losing control of the plane, made the decision to crash it into an open field in rural Pennsylvania rather than risk being overtaken by the passengers. At

10:03 AM EDT, Flight 93 slammed into a reclaimed strip mine near Shanksville, Pennsylvania, at a speed of approximately 580 miles per hour, killing all 44 people on board.

Profiles of the Passengers Who Fought Back Against the Hijackers:

1. Todd Beamer: Todd Beamer was a 32-year-old account manager for Oracle Corporation and a devout Christian. When the hijackers took control of Flight 93, Beamer used an onboard phone to contact GTE operator Lisa Jefferson and informed her of the situation. Beamer then led a group of passengers in an attempt to overpower the hijackers, famously rallying his fellow passengers with the words "Let's roll!" His heroic actions inspired a nation and became a symbol of courage and resilience in the face of adversity.

2. Jeremy Glick: Jeremy Glick was a 31-year-old sales executive and former collegiate judo champion. When the hijackers took control of Flight 93, Glick called his wife, Lyz, and informed her of the situation. He then joined Todd Beamer and other passengers in planning a counterattack against the hijackers. Glick's bravery and selflessness in the face of danger saved countless lives and earned him posthumous accolades for his heroism.

3. Mark Bingham: Mark Bingham was a 31-year-old public relations executive and former collegiate rugby player. When the hijackers took control of Flight 93, Bingham called his mother, Alice Hoglan, and informed her of the situation. He then joined Todd Beamer and other passengers in storming the cockpit and attempting to regain control of the aircraft. Bingham's actions on September 11th saved lives and earned him widespread recognition as a hero.

4. Tom Burnett: Tom Burnett was a 38-year-old senior vice president for a medical devices company. When the hijackers took control of Flight 93, Burnett called his wife, Deena, and informed her of the situation. He then joined Todd Beamer and other passengers in formulating a plan to confront the hijackers and regain control of the aircraft. Burnett's bravery and leadership on September 11th saved lives and inspired countless others to acts of courage.

Legacy of Courage and Sacrifice in Shanksville, Pennsylvania:

The crash of Flight 93 near Shanksville, Pennsylvania, left a lasting impact on the small rural community and the nation as a whole. In the immediate aftermath of the tragedy, local residents rushed to the scene to assist with rescue and recovery efforts, offering food, shelter, and support to first responders and volunteers.

As news of the passengers' heroic actions aboard Flight 93 spread, Shanksville became a symbol of courage and sacrifice in the face of adversity. Memorials and tributes to the passengers and crew of Flight 93 were erected in the area, including the Flight 93 National Memorial, which honors the memory of those who lost their lives in the crash.

Every year on September 11th, people from around the country gather at the Flight 93 National Memorial to pay their respects to the passengers and crew of Flight 93 and to reflect on the events of that fateful day. The memorial serves as a reminder of the bravery and selflessness displayed by ordinary individuals in extraordinary circumstances, and as a testament to the enduring spirit of unity and resilience that binds us together as a nation.

Conclusion:

The story of Flight 93 and the heroes of Shanksville is a powerful reminder of the capacity for courage and sacrifice that lies within each of us. In the face of unimaginable terror and uncertainty, ordinary individuals rose to the occasion and demonstrated extraordinary bravery, ultimately sacrificing their own lives to save others.

Their actions on September 11, 2001, serve as a beacon of hope and inspiration for future generations, reminding us that even in our darkest hour, there is always light to be found in the selfless acts of others. As we honor the memory of the passengers and crew of Flight 93, may we also strive to embody their spirit of courage, resilience, and unity in the face of adversity.

Chapter 6: America Responds

In the wake of the devastating terrorist attacks on September 11, 2001, the United States faced a profound crisis that tested the resilience of its people and institutions. In this chapter, we will explore the immediate response from government agencies and emergency services, President Bush's address to the nation, and the formation of the 9/11 Commission and initial investigations.

Immediate Response from Government Agencies and Emergency Services:

As the events of September 11th unfolded, government agencies and emergency services sprang into action to respond to the unfolding crisis. From local firefighters and police departments to federal agencies and military units, thousands of men and women worked tirelessly to rescue survivors, secure the affected areas, and provide support to those in need.

In New York City, the Fire Department of New York (FDNY) and the New York Police Department (NYPD) mobilized their resources to respond to the attacks on the World Trade Center towers. Despite the chaos and confusion, first responders rushed to the scene, risking their own lives to save others trapped in the burning buildings. Their bravery and selflessness in the face of danger inspired a nation and earned them the title of "heroes of 9/11."

In Washington, D.C., emergency services personnel responded swiftly to the attack on the Pentagon, working alongside military personnel to extinguish fires, treat the injured, and secure the area. The Arlington County Fire Department and other local agencies played a crucial role in containing the blaze and preventing further loss of life, while military personnel provided support and logistical assistance to first responders on the ground.

Across the country, airports, government buildings, and other critical infrastructure were placed on high alert as authorities worked to assess the extent of the threat and prevent further attacks. Law enforcement agencies conducted sweeps of public spaces and transportation hubs, while the Federal Aviation Administration (FAA) grounded all civilian aircraft and implemented enhanced security measures to prevent unauthorized access to airspace.

President Bush's Address to the Nation:

In the hours following the attacks, President George W. Bush addressed the nation from the Oval Office, delivering a message of unity, resolve, and determination in the face of adversity. Standing alongside first responders and members of his administration, President Bush condemned the attacks as acts of cowardice and terrorism, vowing to hold those responsible accountable for their actions.

In his speech, President Bush reassured the American people that the government was taking all necessary measures to ensure their safety and security in the wake of the attacks. He declared a national day of mourning to honor the victims and their families, calling on Americans to come together in solidarity and support one another during this difficult time.

President Bush also outlined the government's response to the attacks, including the deployment of military forces to secure the country's borders and defend against further threats, as well as the initiation of a comprehensive investigation to determine the perpetrators and motives behind the attacks. He pledged to pursue justice for the victims and their families, promising that those responsible would be brought to justice and held accountable for their actions.

Formation of the 9/11 Commission and Initial Investigations:

In the days following the attacks, Congress passed legislation to establish an independent, bipartisan commission to investigate the events of September 11th and make recommendations for preventing future terrorist attacks. The commission, known as the National Commission on Terrorist Attacks Upon the United States, or the 9/11 Commission, was tasked with conducting a thorough inquiry into the circumstances surrounding the attacks, including the intelligence failures and security lapses that allowed them to occur.

Chaired by former New Jersey Governor Thomas Kean and former Indiana Congressman Lee Hamilton, the 9/11 Commission consisted of ten commissioners with diverse backgrounds and expertise in national security, intelligence, law enforcement, and other relevant fields. Over the course of its investigation, the commission held public hearings, interviewed key witnesses, and reviewed thousands of pages of documents to uncover the facts surrounding the attacks and identify areas for improvement in the nation's counterterrorism efforts.

The 9/11 Commission's final report, published in July 2004, provided a comprehensive account of the events leading up to the attacks, including the failures of intelligence agencies to detect and prevent the plot, as well as recommendations for strengthening the country's defenses against future terrorist threats. The report's findings and recommendations served as a roadmap for reforming the nation's intelligence and security apparatus, leading to significant changes in government policies, procedures, and practices aimed at enhancing homeland security and preventing future attacks.

Conclusion:

The immediate response from government agencies and emergency services, President Bush's address to the nation, and the formation of the 9/11 Commission were critical components of America's response to the devastating terrorist attacks of September 11, 2001. In the face of unprecedented challenges and uncertainty, the nation came together to mourn the loss of life, support the victims and their families, and reaffirm its commitment to defending freedom, democracy, and the rule of law.

As we reflect on the events of September 11th and their enduring impact on our country and the world, let us honor the memory of the victims, pay tribute to the bravery and sacrifice of the first responders and emergency personnel, and rededicate ourselves to the values of unity, resilience, and solidarity that define the American spirit.

Chapter 7: Mourning and Unity

In the aftermath of the devastating terrorist attacks on September 11, 2001, the world came together in a collective outpouring of grief, solidarity, and support for the victims and their families. In this chapter, we will explore the national and international expressions of mourning and unity, the memorials and tributes to the victims of 9/11, and the ways in which communities came together in the aftermath of tragedy.

National and International Expressions of Grief and Solidarity:

The attacks of September 11th sent shockwaves around the world, eliciting expressions of grief and solidarity from people of all backgrounds and walks of life. In the United States, Americans gathered in churches, mosques, synagogues, and community centers to mourn the loss of life and pray for healing and peace. Candlelight vigils were held in cities and towns across the country, with people coming together to honor the memory of the victims and offer support to their families and loved ones.

Internationally, world leaders condemned the attacks as acts of cowardice and terrorism and expressed their solidarity with the United States and the victims of 9/11. Countries around the world observed moments of silence and lowered their flags to half-mast in tribute to the victims. In cities from London to Tokyo, people held vigils, lit candles, and laid flowers at makeshift memorials to show their support for the United States and their solidarity with the victims of the attacks.

The attacks of September 11th also inspired acts of kindness and compassion around the world, as people reached out to one another in gestures of solidarity and support. Blood donation drives were organized in cities across the United States, with thousands of people lining up to donate blood to help the victims of the attacks. Charitable organizations raised millions of dollars in donations to provide aid and assistance to those affected by the tragedy, offering financial support, counseling services, and other forms of assistance to help people rebuild their lives in the wake of loss and devastation.

Memorials and Tributes to the Victims of 9/11:

In the years following the attacks, memorials and tributes to the victims of 9/11 were erected in cities and towns across the United States and around the world. These memorials served as places of remembrance and reflection, honoring the memory of the nearly 3,000 people who lost their lives on that fateful day and providing solace and comfort to their families and loved ones.

One of the most iconic memorials to the victims of 9/11 is the National September 11 Memorial & Museum in New York City, located at the site of the World Trade Center towers. The memorial features two reflecting pools, each situated within the footprint of one of the Twin Towers, surrounded by bronze panels inscribed with the names of the victims. The museum, located beneath the memorial, houses artifacts, photographs, and personal stories that commemorate the events of September 11th and honor the lives lost in the attacks.

In Shanksville, Pennsylvania, the Flight 93 National Memorial honors the memory of the passengers and crew of United Airlines Flight 93, who sacrificed their lives to prevent further loss of life on that fateful day. The memorial features a visitor center, a Wall of Names inscribed with the names of the passengers and crew, and a Flight Path Walkway that traces the trajectory of the doomed flight. Visitors to the memorial can pay their respects to the heroes of Flight 93 and learn about their bravery and sacrifice in the face of adversity.

In Washington, D.C., the Pentagon Memorial honors the memory of the 184 people who lost their lives in the attack on the Pentagon. The memorial features 184 illuminated benches, each engraved with the name of a victim, arranged in a pattern that reflects the age and location of each person on the day of the attacks. A landscaped park surrounds the memorial, providing a tranquil space for reflection and remembrance.

Communities Coming Together in the Aftermath of Tragedy:

In the aftermath of the attacks, communities across the United States and around the world came together in a spirit of unity and solidarity to support one another and rebuild in the face of tragedy. Churches, synagogues, mosques, and other religious institutions opened their doors to provide solace and support to those in need, offering counseling services, spiritual guidance, and a sense of community to people struggling to make sense of the senseless violence.

Volunteers from all walks of life came forward to lend a helping hand, assisting with rescue and recovery efforts, providing meals and shelter to first responders and displaced families, and offering comfort and companionship to those grieving the loss of loved ones. From firefighters and police officers to medical professionals and ordinary citizens, people from all backgrounds and professions joined together to offer their support and solidarity to the victims of 9/11 and their families.

In the years following the attacks, communities continued to come together to honor the memory of the victims and ensure that their legacy would never be forgotten. Annual commemorations and remembrance ceremonies were held in cities and towns across the country, bringing people together to pay their respects and reflect on the events of September 11th. These gatherings served as reminders of the enduring spirit of unity and resilience that emerged in the aftermath of tragedy, and as a testament to the power of compassion and solidarity to overcome even the darkest of times.

Conclusion:

The attacks of September

11, 2001, were a defining moment in American history, forever altering the course of the nation and the world. In the face of unimaginable loss and devastation, people from all walks of life came together in a spirit of unity and solidarity to support one another and rebuild in the aftermath of tragedy.

The national and international expressions of grief and solidarity, the memorials and tributes to the victims of 9/11, and the communities that came together in the aftermath of tragedy serve as powerful reminders of the resilience of the human spirit and the capacity for compassion and solidarity to overcome even the greatest of challenges. As we honor the memory of the victims and reflect on the events of September 11th, may we also renew our commitment to building a world of peace, tolerance, and understanding, where the lessons of the past serve as a beacon of hope for the future.

Chapter 8: The War on Terror Begins

In the wake of the devastating terrorist attacks on September 11, 2001, the United States launched a comprehensive military and diplomatic campaign to combat terrorism and hold those responsible for the attacks accountable. This chapter will delve into the U.S. military response in Afghanistan and the hunt for Osama bin Laden, the implementation of security measures and changes in foreign policy, and the impact of 9/11 on civil liberties and public perception.

U.S. Military Response in Afghanistan and the Hunt for Osama bin Laden:

Within weeks of the September 11th attacks, the United States initiated Operation Enduring Freedom, a military campaign aimed at dismantling the al-Qaeda terrorist network and ousting the Taliban regime in Afghanistan, which had provided sanctuary to Osama bin Laden and his associates. The U.S.-led coalition launched airstrikes against Taliban and al-Qaeda targets, while simultaneously deploying Special Forces units on the ground to conduct covert operations and gather intelligence.

The primary objective of Operation Enduring Freedom was to disrupt and degrade al-Qaeda's operational capabilities, dismantle its infrastructure, and capture or kill its leadership, including Osama bin Laden. The United States and its coalition partners worked closely with Afghan forces and local militias to target terrorist training camps, hideouts, and supply routes, while also providing humanitarian assistance and support for the fledgling Afghan government.

The hunt for Osama bin Laden, the mastermind behind the September 11th attacks, became a top priority for U.S. intelligence and military forces. Bin Laden, who had evaded capture for years, was believed to be hiding in the rugged mountainous terrain along the Afghanistan-Pakistan border, making him a difficult target to track and apprehend. U.S. Special Forces and intelligence agencies launched a relentless manhunt, conducting raids, surveillance operations, and drone strikes in an effort to locate and neutralize the elusive terrorist leader.

After months of intense searching, Osama bin Laden was finally located and killed by U.S. Navy SEALs during a daring raid on his compound in Abbottabad, Pakistan, on May 2, 2011. The successful operation, codenamed Operation Neptune Spear, dealt a significant blow to al-Qaeda and marked a major victory in the global war on terror. Bin Laden's death was hailed as a triumph of justice and a milestone in the fight against terrorism, but it also underscored the challenges and complexities of waging war in the shadows against a diffuse and resilient enemy.

Implementation of Security Measures and Changes in Foreign Policy:

In the aftermath of the September 11th attacks, the United States implemented a series of security measures and changes in foreign policy aimed at preventing future terrorist attacks and enhancing national security. These measures included the passage of the USA PATRIOT Act, which expanded the government's surveillance powers, strengthened anti-terrorism laws, and enhanced cooperation between law enforcement and intelligence agencies.

The USA PATRIOT Act, enacted in October 2001, granted federal authorities sweeping new powers to track and monitor suspected terrorists, including the ability to conduct warrantless wiretaps, access financial records, and detain individuals without due process. While the law was initially hailed as a necessary tool in the fight against terrorism, it also raised concerns about government overreach and the erosion of civil liberties.

In addition to domestic security measures, the United States also pursued a more assertive and interventionist foreign policy aimed at confronting terrorist threats and promoting democracy and stability in the Middle East and beyond. The Bush administration adopted a policy of preemption, which justified the use of military force to prevent perceived threats to U.S. national security, as demonstrated by the invasion of Iraq in 2003.

The decision to invade Iraq was based on the belief that Iraqi dictator Saddam Hussein possessed weapons of mass destruction and harbored ties to terrorist organizations, including al-Qaeda. However, the intelligence used to justify the invasion later proved to be flawed, and no evidence of weapons of mass destruction was found. The war in Iraq, which lasted nearly nine years and cost thousands of lives, remains a highly controversial and divisive chapter in U.S. history, with critics questioning the legitimacy and wisdom of the decision to invade.

Impact of 9/11 on Civil Liberties and Public Perception:

The September 11th attacks had a profound impact on civil liberties and public perception in the United States, as concerns about national security and the threat of terrorism led to increased government surveillance, restrictions on individual freedoms, and heightened levels of fear and suspicion. The passage of the USA PATRIOT Act, along with other security measures, raised concerns about government overreach and the erosion of privacy rights, as law enforcement agencies were granted expanded powers to monitor and investigate suspected terrorists.

In the years following 9/11, Muslims, Arabs, and individuals perceived to be of Middle Eastern descent faced heightened levels of discrimination, harassment, and profiling, as fears of terrorism fueled xenophobia and intolerance. Hate crimes against Muslim Americans and mosques surged in the wake of the attacks, reflecting a broader climate of fear and mistrust in the aftermath of 9/11.

The media played a significant role in shaping public perception and attitudes towards terrorism and national security in the post-9/11 era, with sensationalized coverage often fueling fear and hysteria. Images of the attacks, along with constant news updates and warnings of future threats, created a sense of unease and vulnerability among the American public, leading to calls for increased vigilance and security measures.

Despite the challenges and uncertainties of the post-9/11 world, the attacks also inspired acts of resilience, unity, and compassion as communities came together to support one another and rebuild in the aftermath of tragedy. From the heroic efforts of first responders and volunteers to the outpouring of support for victims and their families, the spirit of solidarity and resilience that emerged in the wake of 9/11 served as a powerful reminder of the strength and resilience of the American people.

Conclusion:

The September 11th attacks marked a turning point in American history, ushering in a new era of conflict, insecurity, and uncertainty. The U.S. military response in Afghanistan and the hunt for Osama bin Laden, the implementation of security measures and changes in foreign policy, and the impact of 9/11 on civil liberties and public perception were all defining features of the post-9/11 landscape.

As the United States grappled with the challenges of terrorism and global instability in the years following the attacks, it also reaffirmed its commitment to defending freedom, democracy, and the rule of law in the face of adversity. The lessons of 9/11 continue to shape America's approach to national security and foreign policy, serving as a reminder of the enduring importance of vigilance, resilience, and unity in the fight against terrorism.

Chapter 9: Healing and Rebuilding

The aftermath of the September 11, 2001 attacks left scars that would take years to heal. However, amid the devastation and loss, stories of recovery, resilience, and rebuilding emerged as survivors, families, and communities came together to navigate the long road to healing. In this chapter, we will explore the stories of recovery and resilience among survivors and their families, the rebuilding efforts at Ground Zero and the Pentagon, and the long-term psychological effects on individuals and communities.

Stories of Recovery and Resilience Among Survivors and Their Families:

In the aftermath of the attacks, survivors and their families faced unimaginable challenges as they struggled to come to terms with the loss of loved ones, navigate physical and emotional injuries, and rebuild their lives from the ground up. Yet, amid the grief and pain, stories of resilience, courage, and hope emerged as individuals and families found strength in each other and in their communities.

One such story is that of Lauren Manning, who was severely burned while entering the North Tower of the World Trade Center on the morning of September 11th. Despite sustaining third-degree burns on over 80% of her body, Manning miraculously survived the attack and embarked on a long and arduous journey of recovery. With the support of her family, friends, and medical team, Manning underwent numerous surgeries and intensive rehabilitation to rebuild her body and reclaim her life. Today, she serves as a source of inspiration and hope for other survivors as she continues to advocate for burn victims and raise awareness about the long-term effects of traumatic injuries.

Another remarkable story of resilience is that of the FealGood Foundation, founded by John Feal, a construction worker who lost part of his foot while working at Ground Zero in the aftermath of the attacks. Determined to help other first responders who were injured or became ill as a result of their work at Ground Zero, Feal founded the FealGood Foundation to provide financial assistance, advocacy, and support to those in need. Through his tireless efforts,

Feal has helped secure healthcare benefits and compensation for thousands of 9/11 responders and survivors, ensuring that their sacrifices are never forgotten.

Rebuilding Efforts at Ground Zero and the Pentagon:

In the years following the attacks, efforts to rebuild and revitalize the sites of the World Trade Center and the Pentagon became symbols of resilience and renewal in the face of tragedy. At Ground Zero in New York City, the Lower Manhattan Development Corporation (LMDC) spearheaded the redevelopment of the World Trade Center site, working closely with architects, urban planners, and community stakeholders to create a fitting memorial and vibrant mixed-use complex that would honor the memory of the victims and revitalize the surrounding neighborhood.

The centerpiece of the redevelopment efforts at Ground Zero is the 9/11 Memorial & Museum, which opened to the public on September 11, 2011. The memorial features two reflecting pools set within the footprints of the Twin Towers, surrounded by bronze panels inscribed with the names of the nearly 3,000 people killed in the attacks. The museum, located beneath the memorial, houses artifacts, photographs, and personal stories that commemorate the events of September 11th and honor the lives lost in the attacks.

In addition to the memorial and museum, the redevelopment of the World Trade Center site includes the construction of One World Trade Center, also known as the Freedom Tower, which stands as a symbol of resilience and defiance against terrorism. Completed in 2014, One World Trade Center is the tallest building in the Western Hemisphere and serves as a powerful testament to the strength and resilience of the American people.

Similarly, at the Pentagon in Arlington, Virginia, efforts to rebuild and restore the site of the attack were undertaken with a sense of urgency and purpose. In the months following the attacks, workers labored tirelessly to repair the damage caused by the impact of American Airlines Flight 77 and to restore the Pentagon to its pre-9/11 condition. Despite the challenges posed by the extensive damage and logistical constraints, the Pentagon was fully operational within a year of the attacks, a testament to the resilience and determination of the military and civilian personnel who worked tirelessly to rebuild in the aftermath of tragedy.

Long-Term Psychological Effects on Individuals and Communities:

The psychological toll of the September 11th attacks extended far beyond the physical devastation, leaving lasting scars on individuals, families, and communities. In the years following the attacks, survivors, first responders, and others directly impacted by the events of 9/11 grappled with a range of emotional and psychological challenges, including post-traumatic stress disorder (PTSD), depression, anxiety, and survivor's guilt.

For many survivors and family members of victims, the process of grieving and healing was complicated by feelings of anger, confusion, and disbelief as they struggled to make sense of the senseless violence and loss. Counseling services, support groups, and mental health resources were made available to those in need, but the stigma surrounding mental illness and trauma often made it difficult for individuals to seek help or talk openly about their experiences.

The long-term psychological effects of the attacks also extended to communities and the broader population, as fears of terrorism, uncertainty about the future, and feelings of vulnerability and insecurity pervaded daily life. The constant threat of future attacks, coupled with heightened security measures and a pervasive sense of unease, contributed to a climate of fear and anxiety that lingered in the years following 9/11.

Despite the challenges and hardships faced by individuals and communities in the aftermath of the attacks, stories of resilience, hope, and healing also emerged as people came together to support one another and rebuild in the face of adversity. From volunteer organizations and community outreach programs to acts of kindness and solidarity, the spirit of unity and compassion that emerged in the wake of 9/11 served as a powerful reminder of the strength and resilience of the human spirit.

Conclusion:

The aftermath of the September 11th attacks was marked by stories of recovery, resilience, and rebuilding as survivors, families, and communities came together to navigate the long road to healing. Despite the profound loss and devastation wrought by the attacks, individuals and communities found strength in each other and in their shared commitment to honoring the memory of the victims and rebuilding in the face of adversity.

Through their courage, determination, and compassion, survivors, first responders, and others directly impacted by the events of 9/11 demonstrated the resilience of the human spirit and the power of hope to overcome even the darkest of times. As we reflect on the stories of recovery and resilience in the aftermath of 9/11, may we also renew our commitment to supporting and uplifting those affected by tragedy, and to building a world of peace, tolerance, and understanding where the lessons of the past serve as a beacon of hope for the future.

Chapter 10: Remembering the Fallen

The tragic events of September 11, 2001, claimed the lives of nearly 3,000 innocent people from diverse backgrounds and walks of life. Among the victims were men, women, and children of all ages, representing a multitude of nationalities, religions, and professions. In this chapter, we will honor the memory of the fallen by sharing profiles of some of the victims, highlighting their unique stories, contributions, and the enduring impact of their loss. We will also explore the stories of heroism and sacrifice among first responders, and reflect on the human cost of 9/11 and its lasting legacy.

Profiles of Victims from Diverse Backgrounds and Walks of Life:

1. Betty Ong: Betty Ong was a flight attendant aboard American Airlines Flight 11, the first plane to be hijacked on September 11th. Despite the chaos and danger onboard, Ong remained calm and composed as she relayed crucial information to ground personnel about the unfolding situation. Her courage and quick thinking helped authorities understand the gravity of the attacks and take swift action to prevent further tragedy.

2. Welles Crowther: Welles Crowther, known as the "Man in the Red Bandana," was an equities trader who worked on the 104th floor of the South Tower of the World Trade Center. After the attacks, Crowther helped lead several survivors to safety before returning to the burning building to assist others in need. He ultimately lost his life when the South Tower collapsed, but his bravery and selflessness saved the lives of at least ten people that day.

3. Mohammad Salman Hamdani: Mohammad Salman Hamdani was a Pakistani-American Muslim who worked as a research assistant at Rockefeller University and served as a part-time emergency medical technician (EMT) with the New York City Police Department. On September 11th, Hamdani rushed to the World Trade Center to offer his assistance, despite the risks to his own safety. His remains were found in the rubble of the North Tower, and he was posthumously honored as a hero for his bravery and sacrifice.

4. Lorraine Bay: Lorraine Bay was a mother of three and a devoted wife who worked as an executive assistant at Cantor Fitzgerald on the 105th floor of the North Tower. On the morning of September 11th, Bay called her husband to say goodbye and express her love for her family before the tower collapsed. Her tragic death left a void in the lives of her loved ones, but her memory lives on in the hearts of those who knew and cherished her.

5. Manuel Del Valle Jr.: Manuel Del Valle Jr. was a firefighter with Engine Company 5 in New York City and a dedicated public servant who risked his life to save others on September 11th. Despite the dangers posed by the collapsing towers, Del Valle Jr. bravely entered the North Tower multiple times to rescue survivors and extinguish fires. Tragically, he perished when the tower collapsed, but his legacy of courage and sacrifice lives on in the hearts of his fellow firefighters and the communities he served.

Stories of Heroism and Sacrifice Among First Responders:

1. The Firefighters of FDNY: The Fire Department of New York (FDNY) responded heroically to the attacks on the World Trade Center, with hundreds of firefighters rushing into the burning towers to rescue survivors and extinguish fires. Despite the dangers and uncertainties they faced, these brave men and women worked tirelessly to save lives and protect their fellow citizens. Many firefighters made the ultimate sacrifice that day, losing their lives in the line of duty, but their courage and selflessness continue to inspire future generations of first responders.

2. The Police Officers of NYPD: The New York Police Department (NYPD) also played a crucial role in responding to the attacks and maintaining order in the aftermath of the chaos. Officers worked tirelessly to evacuate civilians, secure the affected areas, and provide support to first responders. Many police officers exhibited extraordinary bravery and heroism, risking their own lives to save others and protect their communities. Their unwavering dedication and sacrifice exemplify the finest traditions of law enforcement and serve as a testament to the resilience of the human spirit.

3. The Emergency Medical Technicians (EMTs) and Paramedics: EMTs and paramedics from across the city responded heroically to the scenes of

devastation, providing emergency medical care to survivors and transporting the injured to hospitals. Despite the risks to their own safety, these dedicated healthcare professionals worked tirelessly to triage patients, administer lifesaving treatments, and comfort those in need. Their swift and selfless actions helped save countless lives in the chaotic aftermath of the attacks, demonstrating the importance of skilled medical personnel in times of crisis.

Reflections on the Human Cost of 9/11 and Its Enduring Impact:

The events of September 11, 2001, exacted a heavy toll on the lives of countless individuals, families, and communities, leaving scars that would take years to heal. The loss of so many innocent lives, the destruction of iconic landmarks, and the senseless violence of the attacks shook the nation to its core and left an indelible mark on the collective consciousness.

For the families and loved ones of the victims, the pain of loss is felt deeply and acutely, as they grapple with the absence of those they cherished and the void left by their untimely deaths. The human cost of 9/11 is immeasurable, with each victim representing a unique story, a cherished life, and a legacy of love and kindness that lives on in the hearts of those who knew them.

Yet, amid the darkness and despair, stories of resilience, heroism, and hope emerged as survivors, families, and communities came together to support one another and rebuild in the aftermath of tragedy. From the bravery of first responders to the outpouring of support from people around the world, the spirit of unity and solidarity that emerged in the wake of 9/11 serves as a powerful reminder of the strength and resilience of the human spirit.

As we reflect on the lives lost and the sacrifices made on September 11th, may we honor the memory of the fallen by striving to build a world of peace, tolerance, and understanding, where the lessons of the past serve as a beacon of hope for the future. May we never forget the heroes who gave their lives to save others, and may their legacy inspire us to work towards a brighter tomorrow for generations to come.

In conclusion, the stories of the victims and heroes of September 11, 2001, serve as a poignant reminder of the human cost of terrorism and the enduring resilience of the human spirit in the face of adversity. As we remember the fallen and honor their memory, may we also renew our commitment to building a world free from fear, hatred, and violence, where all people can live in peace and security.

Chapter 11: Lessons Learned

The events of September 11, 2001, revealed profound failures and shortcomings in intelligence, security, and counterterrorism efforts that allowed the deadliest terrorist attack in history to occur on American soil. In the aftermath of 9/11, policymakers, intelligence agencies, and national security experts conducted a comprehensive analysis to understand the failures that led to the attacks and implemented sweeping changes to prevent similar tragedies from happening in the future. This chapter will delve into the analysis of intelligence failures and security lapses leading up to 9/11, the changes in counterterrorism strategy and national security apparatus, and ongoing efforts to prevent future terrorist attacks.

Analysis of Intelligence Failures and Security Lapses Leading Up to 9/11:

In the years preceding the September 11th attacks, U.S. intelligence agencies received numerous warnings and indicators of an impending terrorist threat, but a series of systemic failures and missteps prevented those warnings from being effectively acted upon. Key intelligence agencies, including the CIA, FBI, and NSA, failed to share critical information, connect the dots, and recognize the gravity of the threat posed by al-Qaeda and its leader, Osama bin Laden.

One of the most significant intelligence failures leading up to 9/11 was the failure to recognize and act upon the intelligence warnings that indicated an imminent terrorist attack. In the months and years prior to 9/11, the CIA received multiple reports of suspicious activities, including the presence of al-Qaeda operatives in the United States, indications of terrorist planning and preparations, and intercepted communications suggesting an attack was imminent. However, these warnings were not effectively communicated to other agencies or translated into actionable intelligence, resulting in a failure to prevent the attacks.

Additionally, there were critical breakdowns in information sharing and coordination between intelligence agencies, both domestically and internationally, that hindered efforts to detect and disrupt terrorist plots. The failure to connect the dots and share information across agency boundaries prevented analysts from piecing together a comprehensive picture of the evolving terrorist threat, leaving critical gaps in the nation's defenses.

Furthermore, the U.S. government's counterterrorism efforts were hampered by bureaucratic infighting, turf battles, and a lack of accountability and oversight. Interagency rivalries and jurisdictional disputes impeded collaboration and cooperation between intelligence agencies, hindering the effectiveness of counterterrorism operations and leaving the country vulnerable to attack.

Changes in Counterterrorism Strategy and National Security Apparatus:

In the wake of the 9/11 attacks, the U.S. government embarked on a comprehensive overhaul of its counterterrorism strategy and national security apparatus to address the failures and shortcomings exposed by the attacks. These reforms encompassed changes to intelligence gathering and analysis, information sharing and coordination, law enforcement and military capabilities, and foreign policy and diplomacy.

One of the most significant changes in counterterrorism strategy was the creation of the Department of Homeland Security (DHS), a new federal agency tasked with coordinating and integrating the nation's efforts to prevent and respond to terrorist threats. Established in November 2002, DHS brought together 22 federal agencies under one umbrella, streamlining the coordination of counterterrorism activities and improving information sharing and collaboration between agencies.

Additionally, the U.S. government implemented reforms to improve intelligence gathering, analysis, and dissemination, including the establishment of the Office of the Director of National Intelligence (ODNI) to oversee the nation's intelligence agencies and improve coordination and integration of intelligence activities. The ODNI was created in response to recommendations made by the 9/11 Commission, which identified failures in intelligence sharing and coordination as key factors contributing to the attacks.

Furthermore, the U.S. government enhanced its counterterrorism capabilities and resources, investing in new technologies, training programs, and intelligence tools to better detect, disrupt, and respond to terrorist threats. This included the expansion of surveillance capabilities, the development of advanced analytical tools and algorithms, and the recruitment and training of specialized counterterrorism personnel.

Ongoing Efforts to Prevent Future Terrorist Attacks:

Despite the significant reforms and improvements made in the aftermath of 9/11, the threat of terrorism remains a persistent and evolving challenge that requires constant vigilance and adaptation. The United States continues to face threats from a diverse array of terrorist groups and actors, including Islamist extremists, domestic extremists, and state-sponsored actors, who seek to inflict harm and sow chaos.

In response to these ongoing threats, the U.S. government has implemented a multi-faceted approach to counterterrorism that includes intelligence gathering and analysis, law enforcement and military action, diplomatic engagement, and international cooperation. The United States works closely with allies and partners around the world to share information, coordinate actions, and disrupt terrorist networks and activities wherever they may be.

Additionally, the U.S. government has invested in efforts to address the underlying drivers of terrorism, including poverty, inequality, political instability, and social grievances, through initiatives aimed at promoting economic development, good governance, human rights, and the rule of law. By addressing the root causes of extremism and building resilience in vulnerable communities, the United States seeks to prevent individuals from being radicalized and recruited by terrorist organizations.

Furthermore, the United States has strengthened its homeland security measures and critical infrastructure protections to mitigate the risk of terrorist attacks on U.S. soil. This includes enhanced screening and security measures at airports and transportation hubs, increased cybersecurity protections for government and private sector networks, and investments in emergency preparedness and response capabilities.

Conclusion:

The events of September 11, 2001, represented a wake-up call for the United States and the international community, highlighting the grave threats posed by terrorism and the need for comprehensive and coordinated efforts to prevent future attacks. In the years following 9/11, the United States implemented significant reforms and changes to its counterterrorism strategy and national security apparatus to address the failures and shortcomings exposed by the attacks.

While progress has been made in strengthening defenses and disrupting terrorist networks, the threat of terrorism remains a persistent and evolving challenge that requires sustained and concerted efforts from governments, law enforcement agencies, intelligence services, and civil society. By learning from the lessons of 9/11, adapting to new threats, and working together collaboratively and proactively, the United States and its allies can continue to prevent terrorist attacks, protect innocent lives, and uphold the values of freedom, democracy, and human rights.

Chapter 12: Memorializing 9/11

The tragic events of September 11, 2001, left an indelible mark on the collective consciousness of the United States and the world. In the years following the attacks, efforts to memorialize and commemorate the lives lost and the heroes who emerged amidst the devastation took on many forms, from solemn ceremonies and tributes to the creation of permanent memorials and museums. In this chapter, we will explore the evolution of memorials and commemorations in the years following 9/11, the design and construction of the National September 11 Memorial & Museum, and the role of art, literature, and media in preserving the memory of 9/11.

Evolution of Memorials and Commemorations:

In the immediate aftermath of the September 11th attacks, makeshift memorials and impromptu vigils sprung up in cities and towns across the country as people sought solace and solidarity in the face of tragedy. These spontaneous displays of remembrance served as a testament to the resilience and unity of the American people in the wake of unspeakable loss.

As time passed, the need for more permanent and formal memorials became apparent, leading to the creation of dedicated spaces and structures to honor the memory of the victims and preserve the legacy of 9/11. From simple monuments and plaques to elaborate sculptures and gardens, memorials to the victims of 9/11 took on a variety of forms, each reflecting the unique spirit and character of the communities they served.

One of the earliest and most iconic memorials to the victims of 9/11 is the "Tribute in Light," an annual art installation that projects two beams of light into the night sky from the site of the World Trade Center in New York City. The Tribute in Light, first displayed in March 2002, has become a symbol of hope and resilience, illuminating the night sky as a beacon of remembrance for the lives lost on September 11th.

In addition to physical memorials, commemorative events and ceremonies have played a central role in honoring the memory of 9/11 and paying tribute to the victims and heroes of the attacks. From annual memorial services at Ground

Zero to community-based initiatives and volunteer efforts, these events serve as opportunities for reflection, remembrance, and renewal, bringing together people from all walks of life to honor the legacy of 9/11.

Design and Construction of the National September 11 Memorial & Museum:

Central to the effort to memorialize the victims of 9/11 is the National September 11 Memorial & Museum, located at the World Trade Center site in New York City. Conceived as a place of remembrance, reflection, and education, the memorial and museum serve as lasting tributes to the lives lost and the heroism displayed on September 11, 2001.

The design of the memorial and museum was selected through an international design competition, which attracted entries from architects and designers around the world. The winning design, titled "Reflecting Absence," was conceived by architect Michael Arad and landscape architect Peter Walker, and features two sunken pools set within the footprints of the Twin Towers, surrounded by bronze parapets inscribed with the names of the nearly 3,000 victims of the attacks.

The memorial plaza, opened to the public on September 11, 2011, provides a tranquil and contemplative space for visitors to pay their respects and honor the memory of the victims. The pools, which sit atop the original foundations of the Twin Towers, are adorned with cascading waterfalls that symbolize the void left by the absence of the towers and evoke a sense of loss and renewal.

Adjacent to the memorial plaza is the National September 11 Memorial Museum, which opened to the public on May 21, 2014. The museum, located beneath the memorial plaza, houses artifacts, photographs, personal stories, and interactive exhibits that document the events of September 11th and preserve the memory of the victims and heroes of the attacks. From twisted steel beams and fragments of the World Trade Center to personal belongings and mementos recovered from Ground Zero, the museum's collection serves as a powerful and poignant reminder of the human cost of 9/11.

Role of Art, Literature, and Media in Preserving the Memory of 9/11:

In addition to physical memorials and museums, art, literature, and media have played a crucial role in preserving the memory of 9/11 and ensuring that the stories of the victims and heroes are never forgotten. Artists, writers, filmmakers, and journalists have used their creative talents to capture the impact and significance of the attacks, providing a platform for reflection, remembrance, and healing.

One notable example is the "9/11 Memorial Quilt," a collaborative art project created by artist Faith Ringgold and a team of volunteers in the months following the attacks. The quilt, composed of individual fabric squares commemorating the victims of 9/11, serves as a powerful symbol of unity and solidarity, bringing together people from all walks of life to honor the memory of the fallen.

Literature has also played a crucial role in preserving the memory of 9/11 and documenting the experiences of survivors, first responders, and witnesses. From memoirs and oral histories to novels and poetry collections, writers have grappled with the complexities of the attacks and their aftermath, offering readers insight into the human toll of terrorism and the resilience of the human spirit.

Similarly, film and television have provided a platform for filmmakers and documentarians to explore the events of 9/11 and their impact on individuals and society. From acclaimed documentaries like "9/11" and "Man on Wire" to fictional dramas like "United 93" and "World Trade Center," filmmakers have sought to capture the emotions, struggles, and triumphs of those affected by the attacks, ensuring that their stories are remembered and honored for generations to come.

Conclusion:

The efforts to memorialize and commemorate the victims and heroes of 9/11 are ongoing, as communities, institutions, and individuals continue to find new and innovative ways to honor the memory of those lost and preserve the legacy of the attacks. From physical memorials and museums to art, literature, and media, the collective response to 9/11 reflects a commitment to remembrance, resilience, and renewal in the face of tragedy.

As we reflect on the events of September 11, 2001, and their enduring impact on our world, may we draw strength from the stories of the victims and heroes who emerged amidst the devastation, and may we honor their memory by working together to build a future free from fear, hatred, and violence. Through remembrance and reflection, may we ensure that the lessons of 9/11 are never forgotten, and that the spirit of unity and compassion that emerged in its aftermath continues to inspire us to strive for a better, more peaceful world.

Chapter 13: Global Implications

The events of September 11, 2001, not only reshaped the landscape of American society but also had far-reaching implications for international relations, geopolitics, and the global fight against terrorism. In this chapter, we will explore the impact of 9/11 on international relations and geopolitics, the spread of terrorism and extremism in the post-9/11 world, and the responses from allies and adversaries to the events of September 11.

Impact of 9/11 on International Relations and Geopolitics:

The attacks of September 11th marked a turning point in international relations, ushering in a new era of global security concerns and reshaping the geopolitical landscape. The United States, as the primary target of the attacks, embarked on a comprehensive campaign to combat terrorism and root out extremist networks around the world, leading to a fundamental shift in U.S. foreign policy priorities.

In the immediate aftermath of 9/11, the Bush administration declared a "War on Terror" and launched military operations in Afghanistan to dismantle the Taliban regime and destroy al-Qaeda's terrorist infrastructure. The invasion of Afghanistan, supported by a coalition of NATO allies and regional partners, marked the beginning of a protracted conflict that would shape the course of U.S. foreign policy for years to come.

The attacks also prompted a reevaluation of traditional notions of sovereignty, security, and international cooperation, as countries around the world grappled with the threat of transnational terrorism and the challenges posed by non-state actors. The concept of preemptive warfare and the use of military force to prevent future terrorist attacks became central tenets of U.S. foreign policy, leading to controversial interventions in Iraq and other parts of the Middle East.

Furthermore, the attacks exacerbated existing tensions and conflicts in the Middle East and fueled anti-American sentiment and extremism in Muslim-majority countries. The U.S. military presence in the region, coupled with perceived injustices and grievances stemming from U.S. foreign policy, provided fertile ground for terrorist recruitment and radicalization, leading to a resurgence of Islamist extremism and violence in the region.

Spread of Terrorism and Extremism in the Post-9/11 World:

The events of September 11th served as a catalyst for the spread of terrorism and extremism in the post-9/11 world, as extremist groups sought to exploit the chaos and instability unleashed by the attacks to advance their own agendas. Al-Qaeda, despite suffering significant losses and setbacks in the years following 9/11, continued to inspire and orchestrate terrorist attacks around the world, including in Europe, Africa, and Southeast Asia.

In addition to al-Qaeda, other terrorist organizations and militant groups emerged or expanded their operations in the wake of 9/11, posing new challenges to global security and stability. Groups like ISIS (Islamic State of Iraq and Syria) and its affiliates capitalized on power vacuums and sectarian tensions in the Middle East to seize territory, establish so-called "caliphates," and carry out brutal acts of violence and terrorism.

The spread of terrorism and extremism in the post-9/11 world was not limited to Islamist groups, however, as other forms of extremism, including far-right extremism and white supremacist terrorism, also emerged as significant threats to global security. The rise of nationalist and populist movements in Europe and the United States, fueled by xenophobia, Islamophobia, and anti-immigrant sentiment, contributed to a resurgence of extremist violence and hate crimes targeting minority communities.

Responses from Allies and Adversaries to the Events of September 11:

In the wake of the September 11th attacks, the United States received an outpouring of support and solidarity from allies and partners around the world, as countries rallied to condemn the terrorist attacks and express their solidarity with the American people. NATO invoked Article 5 of its charter for the first time in its history, declaring that an attack on one member state constituted an attack on all, and pledging to assist the United States in its response to the attacks.

In addition to NATO, other countries and international organizations offered assistance and support to the United States in its efforts to combat terrorism and root out extremist networks. Countries across the globe enacted new counterterrorism laws and measures, bolstered intelligence sharing and cooperation, and contributed troops and resources to multinational military operations in Afghanistan and other theaters of conflict.

However, the response to the events of September 11th was not universally positive, as some countries and actors sought to exploit the situation for their own strategic interests or ideological agendas. Adversarial states like Iran and Syria, for example, provided support and safe haven to terrorist organizations and insurgent groups opposed to U.S. interests in the region, complicating efforts to stabilize and secure conflict-ridden areas.

Furthermore, the U.S.-led interventions in Afghanistan and Iraq, characterized by lengthy and costly military campaigns, sparked widespread controversy and criticism from allies and adversaries alike. Many countries questioned the legality and legitimacy of the wars, citing concerns about civilian casualties, human rights abuses, and the long-term consequences of military intervention for regional stability and security.

Conclusion:

The events of September 11, 2001, had profound and far-reaching implications for international relations, geopolitics, and the global fight against terrorism. The attacks reshaped the strategic landscape of the 21st century, prompting a fundamental reevaluation of traditional notions of security, sovereignty, and international cooperation.

In the two decades since 9/11, the world has grappled with the spread of terrorism and extremism, the rise of non-state actors and transnational threats, and the complexities of navigating an increasingly interconnected and multipolar world. As we reflect on the global implications of 9/11, may we draw lessons from the past to inform our efforts to build a more peaceful, secure, and prosperous world for future generations. Through cooperation, dialogue, and collective action, may we work together to address the root causes of terrorism, promote tolerance and understanding, and uphold the values of freedom, democracy, and human rights.

Chapter 14: 9/11: A Turning Point

The events of September 11, 2001, forever altered the course of American history, leaving an indelible mark on society, culture, and politics. As one of the deadliest terrorist attacks in history, 9/11 served as a stark wake-up call to the United States and the world, prompting profound changes and shaping the national discourse in the years that followed. In this chapter, we will reflect on the significance of 9/11 in American history, examine the changes in society, culture, and politics in the wake of the attacks, and explore the continuing debates over the legacy and meaning of 9/11.

Reflections on the Significance of 9/11 in American History:

The significance of 9/11 in American history cannot be overstated, as the attacks fundamentally altered the nation's sense of security, identity, and place in the world. Prior to 9/11, the United States had enjoyed a period of relative peace and prosperity, with many Americans viewing themselves as insulated from the conflicts and dangers of the outside world. However, the attacks shattered this illusion of invulnerability, exposing the vulnerabilities and insecurities that lay beneath the surface.

In the immediate aftermath of 9/11, the nation grappled with shock, grief, and anger as the full scale of the devastation became apparent. The attacks claimed the lives of nearly 3,000 innocent people from diverse backgrounds and walks of life, including office workers, first responders, and passengers aboard hijacked planes. The loss of life was staggering, and the psychological impact of the attacks reverberated throughout American society, leaving scars that would take years to heal.

Moreover, 9/11 marked a turning point in U.S. foreign policy and military strategy, as the Bush administration declared a "War on Terror" and launched military operations in Afghanistan and later Iraq to combat terrorist networks and rogue regimes believed to pose a threat to national security. The wars in Afghanistan and Iraq, characterized by lengthy tand costly military campaigns, reshaped the geopolitical landscape of the Middle East and strained America's relations with allies and adversaries alike.

Changes in Society, Culture, and Politics in the Wake of the Attacks:

In the wake of 9/11, American society underwent profound changes as fear, uncertainty, and insecurity gripped the nation. The attacks sparked a wave of patriotism and national unity as Americans rallied together in the face of adversity, but they also gave rise to a climate of suspicion, surveillance, and distrust as concerns about terrorism and homeland security dominated the public discourse.

One of the most visible changes in American society following 9/11 was the implementation of heightened security measures and surveillance protocols aimed at preventing future terrorist attacks. Airports, government buildings, and public spaces were subject to increased security screenings and inspections, while law enforcement agencies were granted expanded powers to monitor and investigate potential threats. The passage of the USA PATRIOT Act in October 2001, which granted sweeping new surveillance and law enforcement authorities to federal agencies, marked a significant expansion of government powers in the name of national security.

Furthermore, 9/11 had a profound impact on American culture and popular media, influencing the themes, narratives, and imagery that permeated film, television, literature, and music in the years that followed. The attacks sparked a wave of patriotic sentiment and expressions of solidarity, with artists, musicians, and writers responding to the tragedy in their work and reflecting on its broader implications for American society and identity.

In the realm of politics, the aftermath of 9/11 saw a resurgence of nationalist and populist movements, as politicians sought to capitalize on public fears and anxieties to advance their own agendas. The Bush administration's "War on Terror" rhetoric and policies fueled divisions within the country and abroad, as debates over the use of military force, civil liberties, and the balance between security and freedom dominated the national discourse.

Continuing Debates Over the Legacy and Meaning of

9/11:

Two decades after the attacks, the legacy and meaning of 9/11 continue to be the subject of intense debate and reflection, as scholars, policymakers, and the public grapple with the long-term consequences of the attacks and the response to them. Some view 9/11 as a defining moment in American history, a turning point that ushered in a new era of global insecurity and conflict, while others see it as a tragic but ultimately isolated event that should not overshadow other pressing issues facing society.

One area of ongoing debate is the legacy of the "War on Terror" and the U.S. military interventions in Afghanistan and Iraq. Critics argue that the wars have resulted in immense human suffering, destabilized entire regions, and failed to achieve their stated objectives, while supporters maintain that they were necessary to prevent future terrorist attacks and promote democracy and stability in the Middle East.

Additionally, the events of 9/11 have sparked discussions about the balance between security and civil liberties, as concerns about government surveillance, privacy rights, and due process have come to the forefront of the national debate. The revelation of mass surveillance programs and warrantless wiretapping by the NSA, revealed by whistleblower Edward Snowden in 2013, reignited discussions about the limits of government power and the erosion of constitutional rights in the name of national security.

Moreover, the attacks have raised questions about the nature of terrorism and extremism in the modern world, as policymakers and analysts grapple with the evolving threat landscape and the rise of new challenges, such as cyberterrorism, lone wolf attacks, and domestic extremism. The emergence of groups like ISIS and the resurgence of far-right extremism have underscored the need for a comprehensive and nuanced approach to countering terrorism and extremism in all its forms.

Conclusion:

The events of September 11, 2001, were a watershed moment in American history, leaving an indelible imprint on society, culture, and politics. Two decades later, the legacy of 9/11 continues to shape the national discourse and inform debates about security, liberty, and the future of American democracy. As we reflect on the significance of 9/11, may we honor the memory of the victims and heroes who perished that day, and may we remain vigilant in our efforts to build a more just, inclusive, and resilient society for future generations.

Chapter 15: Looking Forward

As we mark the two-decade anniversary of the September 11th attacks, it is a time for reflection, remembrance, and contemplation of the legacy of that fateful day. In this chapter, we will explore contemporary perspectives on the legacy of 9/11, the challenges and opportunities in the ongoing fight against terrorism, and the hope for a future marked by resilience, unity, and peace.

Contemporary Perspectives on the Legacy of 9/11:

Two decades after the attacks, the legacy of 9/11 continues to shape the world in profound and multifaceted ways. While the immediate aftermath of the attacks saw a surge of unity and solidarity, the long-term impact of 9/11 has been characterized by a complex interplay of social, political, and cultural forces.

One perspective on the legacy of 9/11 is that it marked the beginning of a new era of global insecurity and conflict, as the attacks served as a catalyst for the United States and its allies to launch a series of military interventions in Afghanistan, Iraq, and other parts of the world. The "War on Terror" that followed 9/11 has resulted in significant human suffering, geopolitical upheaval, and the erosion of civil liberties, raising questions about the efficacy and morality of using military force to combat terrorism.

Moreover, the attacks have had a lasting impact on American society, sparking debates about immigration, national security, and the balance between security and civil liberties. The passage of the USA PATRIOT Act and other counterterrorism measures in the wake of 9/11 expanded the powers of the government to surveil, detain, and prosecute suspected terrorists, leading to concerns about privacy rights and due process.

Another perspective on the legacy of 9/11 is that it brought to light the vulnerabilities and inequalities that exist within American society, as the aftermath of the attacks disproportionately affected marginalized communities, including Muslim Americans, immigrants, and people of color. The rise of Islamophobia, hate crimes, and discrimination in the wake of 9/11 underscored the need for greater social cohesion and solidarity in the face of adversity.

Despite the challenges and complexities of the post-9/11 world, there are also signs of resilience, unity, and hope. The outpouring of support and solidarity in the aftermath of the attacks demonstrated the strength of the human spirit and the power of community to overcome tragedy. Moreover, the enduring legacy of 9/11 serves as a reminder of the importance of resilience, compassion, and solidarity in the face of adversity, inspiring individuals and communities to come together to build a brighter future for all.

Challenges and Opportunities in the Ongoing Fight Against Terrorism:

Two decades after 9/11, the fight against terrorism remains a complex and evolving challenge that requires a multifaceted and comprehensive approach. While significant progress has been made in degrading terrorist networks and disrupting their operations, the threat of terrorism continues to evolve and adapt to changing geopolitical dynamics and technological advances.

One of the primary challenges in the ongoing fight against terrorism is the rise of lone wolf actors and self-radicalized individuals who are inspired by extremist ideologies but operate independently of traditional terrorist organizations. These individuals pose a unique and difficult-to-detect threat, as they may not have direct connections to known terrorist groups and can carry out attacks with minimal resources and planning.

Furthermore, the proliferation of digital technology and social media has facilitated the spread of extremist propaganda and recruitment efforts online, enabling terrorist organizations to reach a global audience and radicalize individuals across borders. The use of encrypted messaging platforms and online forums by terrorist groups has made it increasingly difficult for law enforcement and intelligence agencies to monitor and disrupt their activities, posing new challenges to counterterrorism efforts.

Another challenge in the fight against terrorism is the complex geopolitical landscape of the modern world, characterized by regional conflicts, state-sponsored terrorism, and the resurgence of great power competition. The ongoing conflicts in Syria, Yemen, and other parts of the Middle East have provided fertile ground for terrorist groups to operate and recruit new members, while the rivalry between major powers like the United States, Russia, and China has complicated efforts to coordinate international counterterrorism efforts.

Despite these challenges, there are also opportunities for progress and cooperation in the fight against terrorism. Multilateral initiatives such as the Global Counterterrorism Forum and the United Nations Counter-Terrorism Implementation Task Force provide platforms for countries to share best practices, coordinate strategies, and mobilize resources to combat terrorism. International cooperation and intelligence sharing between law enforcement agencies have also proven effective in disrupting terrorist plots and apprehending suspects.

Moreover, efforts to address the root causes of terrorism, including poverty, political instability, and social marginalization, offer long-term solutions to prevent radicalization and extremism from taking hold in vulnerable communities. By promoting education, economic development, and social inclusion, countries can empower individuals and communities to resist the lure of extremist ideologies and build more resilient societies.

Hope for a Future Marked by Resilience, Unity, and Peace:

As we look to the future, there is reason for optimism that the legacy of 9/11 will ultimately be one of resilience, unity, and peace. The events of September 11, 2001, brought people together from all walks of life, transcending differences of race, religion, and nationality, and reminding us of our shared humanity in the face of adversity.

In the two decades since 9/11, we have witnessed countless acts of courage, compassion, and solidarity that have inspired hope and renewed faith in the human spirit. From the heroic actions of first responders on that fateful day to the countless individuals and organizations working tirelessly to promote peace, justice, and reconciliation in the aftermath of tragedy, the legacy of 9/11 is one of resilience, unity, and hope.

Moreover, the lessons learned from the events of 9/11 have served as a catalyst for positive change, inspiring individuals and communities to come together to address the root causes of terrorism and build a more just, inclusive, and peaceful world for future generations. By standing together in solidarity against hate, violence, and extremism, we can honor the memory of the victims and heroes of 9/11 and create a future marked by resilience, unity, and peace.

Don't miss out!

Visit the website below and you can sign up to receive emails whenever Michael Johnson publishes a new book. There's no charge and no obligation.

https://books2read.com/r/B-A-OREFB-VNXAD

Did you love *9/11: America's Day of Terror and Resilience*? Then you should read *The War on Terror*[1] by Michael Johnson!

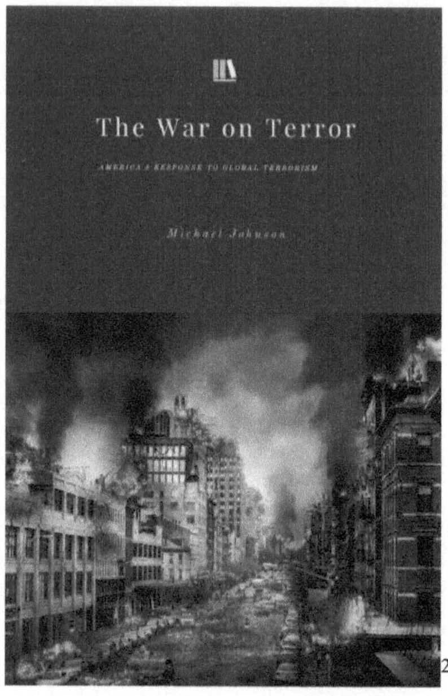

[2]

In this comprehensive analysis, delve into the intricate landscape of modern terrorism, starting from its historical roots to the global repercussions of 9/11. Explore the Bush Doctrine's impact, the controversial interventions in Afghanistan and Iraq, and the evolution of the Global War on Terror. Assess the balance between national security and civil liberties, dissect interrogation tactics, and navigate through shifting strategies under different administrations. From the Arab Spring to the rise of ISIS, from cyber warfare to the Trump era, this book offers critical insights, lessons learned, and future directions in combating terrorism.

---

1. https://books2read.com/u/mYzrXM

2. https://books2read.com/u/mYzrXM

About the Author

Michael Johnson is a distinguished historian specializing in American history. With a degree in History from Harvard University, Johnson's work delves into pivotal moments, figures, and themes shaping the United States. He has authored numerous acclaimed books, offering insightful perspectives and engaging narratives. Johnson's commitment to meticulous scholarship and compelling storytelling has earned him widespread acclaim in the field. Passionate about sharing his expertise, he frequently engages in lectures and public events to foster a deeper appreciation for America's past.

www.ingramcontent.com/pod-product-compliance
Lightning Source LLC
Chambersburg PA
CBHW051828130726
47987CB00003B/1453